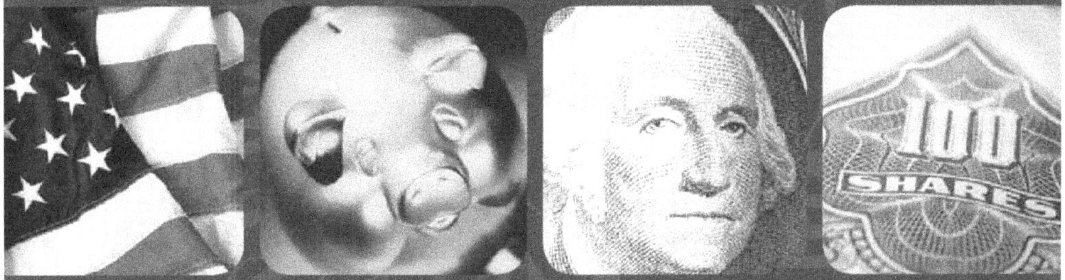

Saving *and* Investing

A Roadmap To Your Financial Security
Through Saving and Investing

U.S. SECURITIES AND EXCHANGE COMMISSION
MCMXXXIV

OFFICE *of* INVESTOR
EDUCATION *and* ADVOCACY

Information is an investor's best tool

Dear Reader

While money doesn't grow on trees, it can grow when you save and invest wisely.

Knowing how to secure your financial well-being is one of the most important things you'll ever need in life. You don't have to be a genius to do it. You just need to know a few basics, form a plan, and be ready to stick to it. No matter how much or little money you have, the important thing is to educate yourself about your opportunities. In this brochure, we'll cover the basics on saving and investing.

At the SEC, we enforce the laws that determine how investments are offered and sold to you. These laws protect investors, but you need to do your part, too. Part of this brochure tells you how to check out investments and the people that sell them so you do not fall victim to fraud or costly mistakes.

No one can guarantee that you'll make money from investments you make. But if you get the facts about saving and investing and follow through with an intelligent plan, you should be able to gain financial security over the years and enjoy the benefits of managing your money.

Please feel free to contact us with any of your questions or concerns about investing. It always pays to learn before you invest. And congratulations on taking your first step on the road to financial security!

U.S. Securities and Exchange Commission
Office of Investor Education and Advocacy
100 F Street, N.E.
Washington, D.C. 20549-0213
Toll-free: (800) SEC-0330
Website: www.investor.gov

Don't Wait to Get Started

YOU CAN DO IT!
IT'S EASIER THAN YOU THINK.

No one is born knowing how to save or to invest. Every successful investor starts with the basics—the information in this brochure.

A few people may stumble into financial security—a wealthy relative may die, or a business may take off. But for most people, the only way to attain financial security is to save and invest over a long period of time.

Time after time, people of even modest means who begin the journey reach financial security and all that it promises: buying a home, educational opportunities for their children, and a comfortable retirement. If they can do it, so can you!

KEYS TO FINANCIAL SUCCESS
1. Make a financial plan.
2. Pay off any high interest debts.
3. Start saving and investing as soon as you've paid off your debts.

Your First Step—Making a Financial Plan

What are the things you want to save and invest for?

- a home
- a car
- an education
- a comfortable retirement
- your children
- medical or other emergencies
- periods of unemployment
- caring for parents

Make your own list and then think about which goals are the most important to you. List your most important goals first.

Decide how many years you have to meet each specific goal, because when you save or invest you'll need to find a savings or

---

YOUR FINANCIAL GOALS

If you don't know where you are going, you may end up somewhere you don't want to be. To end up where you want to be, you'll need a roadmap, a financial plan.

What do you want to save or invest for?   By when?

1. _____   _____

2. _____   _____

3. _____   _____

4. _____   _____

5. _____   _____

---

investment option that fits your time frame for meeting each goal. Many tools exist to help you put your financial plan together.

You'll find a wealth of information, including calculators and links to non-commercial resources at **www.investor.gov**.

KNOW YOUR CURRENT FINANCIAL SITUATION

Sit down and take an honest look at your entire financial situation. You can never take a journey without knowing where you're starting from, and a journey to financial security is no different. You'll need to figure out on paper your current situation—what you own and what you owe. You'll be creating a "net worth statement." On one side of the page, list what you own. These are your "assets." And on the other side list what you owe other people, your "liabilities" or debts.

YOUR NET WORTH STATEMENT			
Assets	**Current Value**	**Liabilities**	**Amount**
Cash	_____	Mortgage balance	_____
Checking accounts	_____	Credit cards	_____
Savings	_____	Bank loans	_____
Cash value of life insurance	_____	Car loans	_____
Retirement accounts	_____	Student loans	_____
Real estate	_____	Other	_____
Home	_____		_____
Other investments	_____		_____
Personal property	_____		_____
TOTAL	_____	**TOTAL**	_____

Subtract your liabilities from your assets. If your assets are larger than your liabilities, you have a "positive" net worth. If your liabilities are greater than your assets, you have a "negative" net worth.

You'll want to update your "net worth statement" every year to keep track of how you are doing. Don't be discouraged if you have a negative net worth. If you follow a plan to get into a positive position, you're doing the right thing.

KNOW YOUR INCOME AND EXPENSES

The next step is to keep track of your income and your expenses for every month. Write down what you and others in your family earn, and then your monthly expenses.

PAY YOURSELF OR YOUR FAMILY FIRST

Include a category for savings and investing. What are you paying yourself every month? Many people get into the habit of saving and investing by following this advice: always pay yourself or your family first. Many people find it easier to pay themselves first if they allow their bank to automatically remove money from their paycheck and deposit it into a savings or investment account.

Likely even better, for tax purposes, is to participate in an employer-sponsored retirement plan such as a 401(k), 403(b), or 457(b). These plans will typically not only automatically deduct money from your paycheck, but will immediately reduce the taxes you are paying. Additionally, in many plans the employer matches some or all of your contribution. When your employer does that, it's offering "free money."

Any time you have automatic deductions made from your paycheck or bank account, you'll increase the chances of being able to stick to your plan and to realize your goals.

FINDING MONEY TO SAVE OR INVEST

If you are spending all your income, and never have money to save or invest, you'll need to look for ways to cut back on your expenses. When you watch where you spend your money, you will be surprised how small everyday expenses that you can do without add up over a year.

KNOW YOUR INCOME AND WHAT YOU SPEND	
Monthly Income	_____
Monthly Expenses	
Savings	_____
Investments	_____
Housing	_____
Rent or mortgage	_____
Electricity	_____
Gas/oil	_____
Telephone	_____
Water/sewer	_____
Property tax	_____
Furniture	_____
Food	_____
Transportation	_____
Loans	_____
Insurance	_____
Education	_____
Recreation	_____
Child care	_____
Health care	_____
Gifts	_____
Other	_____
TOTAL	_____

Small Savings Add Up to Big Money

How much does a cup of coffee cost you?

If you buy a cup of coffee every day for $1.00 (an awfully good price for a decent cup of coffee, nowadays), that adds up to $365.00 a year. If you saved that $365.00 for just one year, and put it into a savings account or investment that earns 5% a year, it would grow to $465.84 by the end of 5 years, and by the end of 30 years, to $1,577.50.

That's the power of "compounding." With compound interest, you earn interest on the money you save and on the interest that money earns. Over time, even a small amount saved can add up to big money.

If you are willing to watch what you spend and look for little ways to save on a regular schedule, you can make money grow. You just did it with one cup of coffee.

If a small cup of coffee can make such a huge difference, start looking at how you could make your money grow if you decided to spend less on other things and save those extra dollars.

If you buy on impulse, make a rule that you'll always wait 24 hours to buy anything. You may lose your desire to buy it after a day. And try emptying your pockets and wallet of spare change at the end of each day. You'll be surprised how quickly those nickels and dimes add up!

PAY OFF CREDIT CARD OR OTHER HIGH INTEREST DEBT

Speaking of things adding up, few investment strategies pay off as well as, or with less risk than, merely paying off all high interest debt you may have.

Many people have wallets filled with credit cards, some of which they've "maxed out" (meaning they've spent up to their credit limit). Credit cards can make it seem easy to buy expensive things when you don't have the cash in your pocket—or in the bank. But credit cards aren't free money.

Most credit cards charge high interest rates—as much as 18 percent or more—if you don't pay off your balance in full each month. If you owe money on your credit cards, the wisest thing you can do is pay off the balance in full as quickly as possible. Virtually no investment will give you the high returns you'll need to keep pace with an 18 percent interest charge. That's why you're better off eliminating all credit card debt before investing savings.

Once you've paid off your credit cards, you can budget your money and begin to save and invest. Here are some tips for avoiding credit card debt:

Put Away the Plastic
Don't use a credit card unless your debt is at a manageable level and you know you'll have the money to pay the bill when it arrives.

Know What You Owe
It's easy to forget how much you've charged on your credit card. Every time you use a credit card, write down how much you have spent and figure out how much you'll have to pay that month. If you know you won't be able to pay your balance in full, try to figure out how much you can pay each month and how long it'll take to pay the balance in full.

Pay Off the Card with the Highest Rate
If you've got unpaid balances on several credit cards, you should first pay down the card that charges the highest rate. Pay as much as you can toward that debt each month until your balance is once again zero, while still paying the minimum on your other cards.

The same advice goes for any other high interest debt (about 8% or above) which does not offer the tax advantages of, for example, a mortgage.

Now, once you have paid off those credit cards and begun to set aside some money to save and invest, what are your choices?

Making Money Grow

THE TWO WAYS TO MAKE MONEY

There are basically two ways to make money.

1. **You work for money.**
   Someone pays you to work for them or you have your own business.

2. **Your money works for you.**
   You take your money and you save or invest it.

YOUR MONEY CAN WORK FOR YOU IN TWO WAYS

Your money earns money. When your money goes to work, it may earn a steady paycheck. Someone pays you to use your money for a period of time. When you get your money back, you get it back plus "interest." Or, if you buy stock in a company that pays "dividends" to shareholders, the company may pay you a portion of its earnings on a regular basis. Your money can make an "income," just like you. You can make more money when you and your money work.

You buy something with your money that could increase in value. You become an owner of something that you hope increases in value over time. When you need your money back, you sell it, hoping someone else will pay you more for it. For instance, you buy a piece of land thinking it will increase in value as more businesses or people move into your town. You expect to sell the land in five, ten, or twenty years when someone will buy it from you for a lot more money than you paid.

And sometimes, your money can do both at the same time—earn a steady paycheck and increase in value.

THE DIFFERENCES BETWEEN SAVING AND INVESTING

Saving

Your "savings" are usually put into the safest places, or products, that allow you access to your money at any time. Savings products include savings accounts, checking accounts, and certificates of deposit. Some deposits in these products may be insured by the Federal Deposit Insurance Corporation or the National Credit Union Administration. But there's a tradeoff for security and ready availability. Your money is paid a low wage as it works for you.

After paying off credit cards or other high interest debt, most smart investors put enough money in a savings product to cover an emergency, like sudden unemployment. Some make sure they have up to six months of their income in savings so that they know it will absolutely be there for them when they need it.

But how "safe" is a savings account if you leave all of your money there for a long time, and the interest it earns doesn't keep up with inflation? What if you save a dollar when it can buy a loaf of bread. But years later when you withdraw that dollar plus the interest you earned on it, it can only buy half a loaf? This is why many people put some of their money in savings, but look to investing so they can earn more over long periods of time, say three years or longer.

Investing

When you "invest," you have a greater chance of losing your money than when you "save." The money you invest in securities, mutual funds, and other similar investments typically is not federally insured. You could lose your "principal"—the amount you've invested. But you also have the opportunity to earn more money.

THE BASIC TYPES OF PRODUCTS	
Savings	**Investments**
Savings accounts	Bonds
Certificates of deposit	Stocks
Checking accounts	Mutual funds
	Real estate
	Commodities (gold, silver, etc.)

What about risk?

All investments involve taking on risk. It's important that you go into any investment in stocks, bonds or mutual funds with a full understanding that you could lose some or all of your money in any one investment. While over the long term the stock market has historically provided around 10% annual returns (closer to 6% or 7% "real" returns when you subtract for the effects of inflation), the long term does sometimes take a rather long, long time to play out. Those who invested all of their money in the stock market at its peak in 1929 (before the stock market crash) would wait over 20 years to see the stock market return to the same level.

However, those that kept adding money to the market throughout that time would have done very well for themselves, as the lower cost of stocks in the 1930s made for some hefty gains for those who bought and held over the course of the next twenty years or more.

It is often said that the greater the risk, the greater the potential reward in investing, but taking on unnecessary risk is often avoidable. Investors best protect themselves against risk by spreading their money among various investments, hoping that if one investment loses money, the other investments will more than make up for those losses. This strategy, called "diversification," can be neatly summed up as, "Don't put all your eggs in one basket." Investors also protect themselves from the risk of investing all their money at the wrong time (think 1929) by following a consistent pattern of adding new money to their investments over long periods of time.

Once you've saved money for investing, consider carefully all your options and think about what diversification strategy makes sense for you. While the SEC cannot recommend any particular investment product, you should know that a vast array of investment products exists—including stocks and stock mutual funds, corporate and municipal bonds, bond mutual funds, certificates of deposit, money market funds, and U.S. Treasury securities.

Diversification can't *guarantee* that your investments won't suffer if the market drops. But it can improve the chances that you won't lose money, or that if you do, it won't be as much as if you weren't diversified.

What are the best investments for me?

The answer depends on when you will need the money, your goals, and if you will be able to sleep at night if you purchase a risky investment where you could lose your principal.

For instance, if you are saving for retirement, and you have 35 years before you retire, you may want to consider riskier investment products, knowing that if you stick to only the "savings" products or to less risky investment products, your money will grow too slowly—or, given inflation and taxes, you may *lose* the purchasing power of your money. A frequent mistake people make is putting money they will not need for a very long time in investments that pay a low amount of interest.

On the other hand, if you are saving for a short-term goal, five years or less, you don't want to choose risky investments, because when it's time to sell, you may have to take a loss. Since investments often move up and down in value rapidly, you want to make sure that you can wait and sell at the best possible time.

When you make an investment, you are giving your money to a company or enterprise, hoping that it will be successful and pay you back with even more money.

Stocks and Bonds

Many companies offer investors the opportunity to buy either stocks or bonds. The example below shows you how stocks and bonds differ.

Let's say you believe that a company that makes automobiles may be a good investment. Everyone you know is buying one of its cars, and your friends report that the company's cars rarely break down and run well for years. You either have an investment professional investigate the company and read as much as possible about it, or you do it yourself.

After your research, you're convinced it's a solid company that will sell many more cars in the years ahead.

The automobile company offers both stocks and bonds. With the bonds, the company agrees to pay you back your initial investment in ten years, plus pay you interest twice a year at the rate of 8% a year.

If you buy the stock, you take on the risk of potentially losing a portion or all of your initial investment if the company does poorly or the stock market drops in value. But you also may see the stock increase in value beyond what you could earn from the bonds. If you buy the stock, you become an "owner" of the company.

You wrestle with the decision. If you buy the bonds, you will get your money back plus the 8% interest a year. And you think the company will be able to honor its promise to you on the bonds because it has been in business for many years and doesn't look like it could go bankrupt. The company has a long history of making cars and you know that its stock has gone up in price by an average of 9% a year, plus it has typically paid stockholders a dividend of 3% from its profits each year.

THE MAIN DIFFERENCES BETWEEN STOCKS AND BONDS	
Stocks	**Bonds**
If the company profits or is perceived as having strong potential, its stock may go up in value and pay dividends. You may make more money than from the bonds.	The company promises to return money plus interest.
Risk: The company may do poorly, and you'll lose a portion or all of your investment.	Risk: If the company goes bankrupt, your money may be lost. But if there is any money left, you will be paid before stockholders.

You take your time and make a careful decision. Only time will tell if you made the right choice. You'll keep a close eye on the company and keep the stock as long as the company keeps selling a quality car that consumers want to drive, and it can make an acceptable profit from its sales.

WHY SOME INVESTMENTS MAKE MONEY AND OTHERS DON'T

You can potentially make money in an investment if:

- The company performs better than its competitors.

- Other investors recognize it's a good company, so that when it comes time to sell your investment, others want to buy it.

- The company makes profits, meaning they make enough money to pay you interest for your bond, or maybe dividends on your stock.

You can lose money if:

- The company's competitors are better than it is.

- Consumers don't want to buy the company's products or services.

- The company's officers fail at managing the business well, they spend too much money, and their expenses are larger than their profits.

- Other investors that you would need to sell to think the company's stock is too expensive given its performance and future outlook.

- The people running the company are dishonest. They use your money to buy homes, clothes, and vacations, instead of using your money on the business.

- They lie about any aspect of the business: claim past or future profits that do not exist, claim it has contracts to sell its products when it doesn't, or make up fake numbers on their finances to dupe investors.

- The brokers who sell the company's stock manipulate the price so that it doesn't reflect the true value of the company. After they pump up the price, these brokers dump the stock, the price falls, and investors lose their money.

- For whatever reason, you have to sell your investment when the market is down.

MUTUAL FUNDS

Because it is sometimes hard for investors to become experts on various businesses—for example, what are the best steel, automobile, or telephone companies—investors often depend on professionals who are trained to investigate companies and recommend companies that are likely to succeed. Since it takes work to pick the stocks or bonds of the companies that have the best chance to do well in the future, many investors choose to invest in mutual funds.

What is a mutual fund?

A mutual fund is a pool of money run by a professional or group of professionals called the "investment adviser." In a managed mutual fund, after investigating the prospects of many companies, the fund's investment adviser will pick the stocks or bonds of companies and put them into a fund.

Investors can buy shares of the fund, and their shares rise or fall in value as the values of the stocks and bonds in the fund rise and fall. Investors may typically pay a fee when they buy or sell their shares in the fund, and those fees in part pay the salaries and expenses of the professionals who manage the fund.

Even small fees can and do add up and eat into a significant chunk of the returns a mutual fund is likely to produce, so you need to look carefully at how much a fund costs and think about how much it will cost you over the amount of time you plan to own its shares. If two funds are similar in every way except that one charges a higher fee than the other, you'll make more money by choosing the fund with the lower annual costs.

For more information about mutual fund fees and expenses, be sure to read our brochure entitled "Invest Wisely: An Introduction to Mutual Funds"—which you can read online at **www.investor.gov** or order for free by calling the Federal Citizen Information Center at **(888) 878-3256**.

MUTUAL FUNDS WITHOUT ACTIVE MANAGEMENT

One way that investors can obtain for themselves nearly the full returns of the market is to invest in an "index fund." This is a mutual fund that does not attempt to pick and choose stocks of individual companies based upon the research of the mutual fund managers or to try to time the market's movements. An index fund seeks to equal the returns of a major stock index, such as the Standard & Poor's 500, the Wilshire 5000, or the Russell 3000. Through computer programmed buying and selling, an index fund tracks the holdings of a chosen index, and so shows the same returns as an index minus, of course, the annual fees involved in running the fund. The fees for index mutual funds generally are much lower than the fees for managed mutual funds.

Historical data shows that index funds have, primarily because of their lower fees, enjoyed higher returns than the average managed mutual fund. But, like any investment, index funds involve risk.

WATCH "TURNOVER" TO AVOID PAYING EXCESS TAXES

To maximize your mutual fund returns, or any investment returns, know the effect that taxes can have on what actually ends up in your pocket. Mutual funds that trade quickly in and out of stocks will have what is known as "high turnover." While selling a stock that has moved up in price does lock in a profit for the fund, this is a profit for which taxes have to be paid. Turnover in a fund creates taxable capital gains, which are paid by the mutual fund shareholders. All mutual funds are now mandated by the SEC to show both their before- and after-tax returns. The differences between what a fund is reportedly earning, and what a fund is earning after taxes are paid on the dividends and capital gains, can be quite striking. If you plan to hold mutual funds in a taxable account, be sure to check out these historical returns in the mutual fund prospectus to see what kind of taxes you might be likely to incur.

Do I Need an Investment Professional?

Are you the type of person who will read as much as possible about potential investments and ask questions about them? If so, maybe you don't need investment advice. But if you're busy with your job, your children, or other responsibilities, or feel you don't know enough about investing on your own, then you may need professional investment advice.

WARNING!
Before You Invest Always Check with the SEC and Your State's Securities Regulator:
Is the investment registered?
Have investors complained about the investment in the past?
Have the people who own or manage the investment been in trouble in the past?
Is the person selling me this investment licensed in my state?
Has that person been in trouble with the SEC, my state, or other investors in the past?

Investment professionals offer a variety of services at a variety of prices. It pays to comparison shop. You can get investment advice from most financial institutions that sell investments, including brokerages, banks, mutual funds, and insurance companies. You can also hire a broker, an investment adviser, an accountant, a financial planner, or other professional to help you make investment decisions.

Some financial planners and investment advisers offer a complete financial plan, assessing every aspect of your financial life and developing a detailed strategy for meeting your financial goals. They may charge you a fee for the plan, a percentage of your assets that they manage, or receive commissions from the companies whose products you buy, or a combination of these. You should know exactly what services you are getting and how much they will cost.

Remember, there is no such thing as a free lunch. Professional financial advisers do not perform their services as an act of charity. If they are working for you, they are getting paid for their efforts. Some of their fees are easier to see immediately than are others. But, in all cases, you should always feel free to ask questions about how and how much your adviser is being paid. And if the fee is quoted to you as a percentage, make sure that you understand what that translates to in dollars.

In contrast to investment advisers, brokers make recommendations about specific investments like stocks, bonds, or mutual funds. While taking into account your overall financial goals, brokers generally do not give you a detailed financial plan. Brokers are generally paid commissions when you buy or sell securities through them. If they sell you mutual funds make sure to ask questions about what fees are included in the mutual fund purchase.

Brokerages vary widely in the quantity and quality of the services they provide for customers. Some have large research staffs, large national operations, and are prepared to service almost any kind of financial transaction you may need. Others are small and may specialize in promoting investments in unproven and very risky companies. And there's everything else in between.

A **discount brokerage** charges lower fees and commissions for its services than what you'd pay at a full-service brokerage. But generally you have to research and choose investments by yourself. A **full-service brokerage** costs more, but the higher fees and commissions pay for a broker's investment advice based on that firm's research.

The best way to choose an investment professional is to start by asking your friends and colleagues who they recommend. Try to get several recommendations, and then meet with potential advisers face-to-face. Make sure you get along. Make sure you understand each other. After all, it's your money.

OPENING A BROKERAGE ACCOUNT

When you open a brokerage account, whether in person or online, you will typically be asked to sign a new account agreement. You should carefully review all the information in this agreement because it determines your legal rights regarding your account.

Do not sign the new account agreement unless you thoroughly understand it and agree with the terms and conditions it imposes on you. Do not rely on statements about your account that are not in this agreement. Ask for a copy of any account documentation prepared for you by your broker.

The broker should ask you about your investment goals and personal financial situation, including your income, net worth, investment experience, and how much risk you are willing to take on. Be honest. The broker relies on this information to determine which investments will best meet your investment goals and tolerance for risk. If a broker tries to sell you an investment before asking you these questions, that's a very bad sign. It signals that the broker has a greater interest in earning a commission than recommending an investment to you that meets your needs. The new account agreement requires that you make three critical decisions:

1. Who will make the final decisions about what you buy and sell in your account?

You will have the final say on investment decisions unless you give "discretionary authority" to your broker. Discretionary authority allows your broker to invest your money without consulting you about the price, the type of security, the amount, and when to buy or sell. Do not give discretionary authority to your broker without seriously considering the risks involved in turning control over your money to another person.

2. How will you pay for your investments?

Most investors maintain a "cash" account that requires payment in full for each security purchase. But if you open a "margin" account, you can buy securities by borrowing money from your broker for a portion of the purchase price. Be aware of the risks involved with buying stocks on margin. Beginning investors generally should not get started with a margin account. Make sure you understand how a margin account works, and what happens in the worst case scenario before you agree to buy on margin. Unlike other loans, like for a car or a home, that allow you to pay back a fixed amount every month, when you buy stocks on margin you can be faced with paying back the entire margin loan all at once if the price of the stock drops suddenly and dramatically. The firm has the authority to immediately sell any security in your account, without notice to you, to cover any shortfall resulting from a decline in the value of your securities. You may owe a substantial amount of money even after your securities are sold. The margin account agreement generally provides that the securities in your margin account may be lent out by the brokerage firm at any time without notice or compensation to you.

3. How much risk should you assume?

In a new account agreement, you must specify your overall investment objective in terms of risk. Categories of risk may have labels such as "income," "growth," or "aggressive growth." Be certain that you fully understand the distinctions among these terms, and be certain that the risk level you choose accurately reflects your age, experience and investment goals. Be sure that the investment products recommended to you reflect the category of risk you have selected.

When opening a new account, the brokerage firm may ask you to sign a legally binding contract to use the arbitration process to settle any future dispute between you and the firm or your sales representative. Signing this agreement means that you give up the right to sue your sales representative and firm in court.

How Can I Protect Myself?

ASK QUESTIONS!

You can never ask a dumb question about your investments and the people who help you choose them, especially when it comes to how much you will be paying for any investment, both in upfront costs and ongoing management fees.

Here are some questions you should ask when choosing an investment professional or someone to help you:

- What training and experience do you have? How long have you been in business?

- What is your investment philosophy? Do you take a lot of risks or are you more concerned about the safety of my money?

- Describe your typical client. Can you provide me with references, the names of people who have invested with you for a long time?

- How do you get paid? By commission? Based on a percentage of assets you manage? Another method? Do you get paid more for selling your own firm's products?

- How much will it cost me in total to do business with you?

Your investment professional should understand your investment goals, whether you're saving to buy a home, paying for your children's education, or enjoying a comfortable retirement.

Your investment professional should *also* understand your tolerance for risk. That is, how much money can you afford to lose if the value of one of your investments declines? An investment professional has a duty to make sure that he or she only recommends investments that are suitable for you. That is, that the investment makes sense for you based on your other securities holdings, your financial situation, your means, and any other information that your investment professional thinks is important. The best investment professional is one who fully understands your objectives and matches investment recommendations to your goals. You'll want someone you can understand, because your investment professional should teach you about investing and the investment products.

How Should I Monitor My Investments?

Investing makes it possible for your money to work for you. In a sense, your money has become your employee, and that makes you the boss. You'll want to keep a close watch on how your employee, your money, is doing.

Some people like to look at the stock quotations every day to see how their investments have done. That's probably too often. You may get too caught up in the ups and downs of the "trading" value of your investment, and sell when its value goes down temporarily—even though the performance of the company is still stellar. Remember, you're in for the long haul.

Some people prefer to see how they're doing once a year. That's probably not often enough. What's best for you will most likely be somewhere in between, based on your goals and your investments.

But it's not enough to simply check an investment's performance. You should compare that performance against an index of similar investments over the same period of time to see if you are getting the proper returns for the amount of risk that you are assuming. You should also compare the fees and commissions that you're paying to what other investment professionals charge.

While you should monitor performance regularly, you should pay close attention *every* time you send your money somewhere else to work.

Every time you buy or sell an investment you will receive a confirmation slip from your broker. Make sure each trade was

IMPORTANT CONTACTS	
SEC	**NASAA**
100 F Street, N.E.	750 First Street, N.E., Suite 1140
Washington, D.C. 20549-0213	Washington, D.C. 20002
Toll-free: (800) SEC-0330	Phone: (202) 737-0900
Website: www.investor.gov	Website: www.nasaa.org

completed according to your instructions. Make sure the buying or selling price was what your broker quoted. And make sure the commissions or fees are what your broker said they would be.

Watch out for unauthorized trades in your account. If you get a confirmation slip for a transaction that you didn't approve beforehand, call your broker. It may have been a mistake. If your broker refuses to correct it, put your complaint in writing and send it to the firm's compliance officer. Serious complaints should always be made in writing.

Remember, too, that if you rely on your investment professional for advice, he or she has an obligation to recommend investments that match your investment goals and tolerance for risk. Your investment professional should not be recommending trades simply to generate commissions. That's called "churning," and it's illegal.

How Can I Avoid Problems?

Choosing someone to help you with your investments is one of the most important investment decisions you will ever make. While most investment professionals are honest and hardworking, you must watch out for those few unscrupulous individuals. They can make your life's savings disappear in an instant.

Securities regulators and law enforcement officials can and do catch these criminals. But putting them in jail doesn't always get your money back. Too often, the money is gone. The good news is you can avoid potential problems by protecting yourself.

Let's say you've already met with several investment professionals based on recommendations from friends and others you trust, and you've found someone who clearly understands your investment objectives. Before you hire this person, you still have more homework.

Make sure the investment professional and her firm are registered with the SEC and licensed to do business in your state. And find out from your state's securities regulator whether the investment professional or her firm have ever been disciplined, or whether they have any complaints against them. You'll find contact information for securities regulators in the U.S. by visiting the website of the North American Securities Administrators Association (NASAA) at www.nasaa.org or by calling (202) 737-0900.

You should also find out as much as you can about any investments that your investment professional recommends.

First, make sure the investments are registered. Keep in mind, however, the mere fact that a company has registered and files reports with the SEC doesn't guarantee that the company will be a good investment.

Likewise, the fact that a company hasn't registered and doesn't file reports with the SEC doesn't mean the company is a fraud. Still, you may be asking for serious losses if, for instance, you invest in a small, thinly traded company that isn't widely known solely on the basis of what you may have read online. One simple phone call to your state regulator could prevent you from squandering your money on a scam.

Be wary of promises of quick profits, offers to share "inside information," and pressure to invest before you have an opportunity to investigate. These are all warning signs of fraud. Ask your investment professional for written materials and prospectuses, and read them before you invest. If you have questions, now is the time to ask.

- How will the investment make money?

- How is this investment consistent with my investment goals?

- What must happen for the investment to increase in value?

- What are the risks?

- Where can I get more information?

Finally, it's always a good idea to write down everything your investment professional tells you. Accurate notes will come in handy if ever there's a problem.

Some investments make money. Others lose money. That's natural, and that's why you need a diversified portfolio to minimize your risk. But if you lose money because you've been cheated, that's not natural, that's a problem.

Sometimes all it takes is a simple phone call to your investment professional to resolve a problem. Maybe there was an honest mistake that can be corrected. If talking to the investment professional doesn't resolve the problem, talk to the firm's manager, and write a letter to confirm your conversation. If that doesn't lead to a resolution, you may have to initiate private legal action. You may need to take action quickly because legal time limits for doing so vary. Your local bar association can provide referrals for attorneys who specialize in securities law.

At the same time, call or write to us and let us know what the problem was. Investor complaints are very important to the SEC. You may think you're the only one experiencing a problem, but typically, you're not alone. Sometimes it takes only one investor's complaint to trigger an investigation that exposes a bad broker or an illegal scheme. Complaints can be filed online with us by going to **www.sec.gov/complaint.shtml**.

Keep in Touch With Us

We hope that you've found this brochure helpful. Please let us know how it can be improved.

We've only covered the basics, and there's a lot more to learn about saving and investing. But you'll be learning as you go and over your lifetime.

As we said at the beginning, the most important thing is to get started. And remember to ask questions as you make your investment decisions.

Be sure to find out if the person is licensed to sell investments, and if the investment is registered with us. So, we look forward to hearing from you. And in the years ahead, let us know how well your money is growing.

U.S. Securities and Exchange Commission
Office of Investor Education and Advocacy
100 F Street, N.E.
Washington, D.C. 20549-0213
Toll-free: (800) SEC-0330
Website: www.investor.gov

To order a copy of this publication, please visit www.pueblo.gsa.gov. To order by phone, call the Federal Citizen Information Center at (888)878-3256 Monday-Friday 8am to 8pm ET.

SEC
OFFICE *of* INVESTOR
EDUCATION *and* ADVOCACY

1-800-732-0330
www.investor.gov